The Real Truth About

Marriage

Divorce

Remarriage

What no one is telling you, but what you desperately need to know!

By Lambert & Kim Sands

Copyright © 2014 Marriage Mechanics Ministries

All rights reserved. No part of this book may be used or reproduced by any means, graphic, electronic, or mechanical, including photocopying, recording, taping or by any information storage retrieval system without the written permission of the publisher except in the case of brief quotations embodied in critical articles and reviews. All Scriptures are taken from the King James Version of the Bible.

Table of Contents

Introduction..........................7

A Real Life Experience......15
Questions Answered...........33
Grace, Grace, God's Grace.......52

Introduction

A gentleman shared a disturbing dream that he had one night. In the dream, he was in a worship service at a large convention of sort. The room was packed to capacity with ministers and pastors of many nations and cultures from around the world. They were in a praise and worship segment of the service and everyone's hands were raised. Tears flowed down many faces as they sang songs of worship before the Lord. Suddenly, he looked up to see what looked like blood dripping from the hands of those in front of him. Feeling a bit uneasy, he turned around and made his way to the back of the room. Again, he looked at the uplifted hands and they were all stained with blood. It was then that he heard a voice say to him, *"Tell my people the truth of my word, or their blood will be on your hands as well."*

Nowhere is the truth more hidden as in the message of marriage, divorce, and remarriage. While thousands are daily taking marriage vows, they are breaking their vows just as quickly because they have not or are not being taught the truth concerning the marriage covenant. The question is asked in Romans 10:14, *"How shall they hear without a preacher?"* Those of us, who have been called to ministry, must realize the awesome responsibility entrusted to us. If we are going to be ministers of God, we must uphold God's word. We don't have a personal message. It is God who gives the message, and we are constrained to carry it to the people. The word of God is a powerful two-edged sword that cuts and wounds, but also heals and restores.

There are some ministers that say the message is too hard, and it will destroy their churches. Others caution, *"Speak about marriage, but do not touch the divorce and remarriage issue."* As we minister this message, we have also been told, *"We will only support you if you change your stance on remarriage."* And we wonder why marriages are a mess, families are being destroyed, children are out of control, and issues of abortion, suicide, and homosexuality have become a flood-tide of immorality.

In the book of Revelation, the churches at Pergamos and Thyatira were confronted for issues of fornication and adultery and told to, *"Repent!"* And, if they didn't repent, there would be dire consequences. The same is true today. If we don't repent, the Lord will bring swift judgment upon us. The church in the Western World is already experiencing the judgment of God as many are dying from disease and other phenomenal occurrences. We must turn now!

Today, in the United States of America, the rate of broken marriages is higher than that of any other nation in the world, and fornication and adultery have become commonly accepted practices. Even pastors are exchanging their old wives for newer ones, or younger ones. Instant gratification is the order of the day. Christians are now asking, *"What is wrong with being married a few times if that is what I want? If my spouse falls short, don't I have the right to get rid of him/her? What if I feel I made a mistake, or I just don't want to be married anymore?"*

Many are crying for the voice of truth that will lead God's people from the scourge of broken marriages and families. Are you a minister, but you do not quite understand what to tell the people concerning marital and relational issues? Are you afraid to speak the unadulterated word of God? Are you willing to speak up where many are sitting silent because of compromise? The Bible says, *"If any of you lack wisdom, let him ask of God, that giveth to all men liberally, and upbraideth not; and it shall be given him. James 1:4."* The Holy Spirit is here to lead and guide us if we would be humble enough to follow him.

Be aware that the time will come when Christians will be required to give their lives for the word of God. If we don't stand up for something now, eventually we will fall for anything. Whether we like it or not, the next doctrinal compromise will be more subtle and demonic in nature. Even now the vile sins of homosexuality and lesbianism are attempting to infiltrate the pulpit. In fact, it is already happening as the pillars of holiness and separation from the world are removed.

Most ministers and congregations are sleeping while this demonic onslaught is besieging the church. Nonetheless, those of us who know and desire the truth must arise. We must arm ourselves with the word of God like never before and fight the good fight of faith. It's not about what we feel is right but what the word of God declares.

We must fight for our marriages and families! We must fight for the souls of men! The world needs to hear our voices loudly and clearly. Let's wake up, sound the alarm, the lives of men and women are at stake! Surely you can look around and see that time is not as long as it has been, Jesus is indeed on his way!

Even so, come Lord Jesus.

*Let not sin therefore reign
in your mortal body,
that ye should obey it
in the lusts thereof.*
Romans 6:12

1.
A Real Life Experience

Cameron and Brenda were married right after graduating college. For a few years all was well, then, the marriage encountered some rocky roads when Cameron found himself in an affair with a co-worker. Brenda was devastated when she learned of the affair, and refused to forgive him. In anger, she filed for a divorce, hoping to start her life over.

Just before her divorce was final, Brenda met Allen. Allen was a successful bachelor who had never been married. Within months, the couple developed a close relationship and eventually they decided to tie the knot. Allen proposed one weekend in a lovely log cabin in Ocoee, Tennessee. Several weeks later, they put together a simple but romantic plan for a lovely wedding.

Wanting to get the counseling done early, they went to a local pastor in search of pre-marital counseling, and the possibility of also having him perform their wedding. Brenda secretly wanted to be sure that what happened in her first marriage was not repeated, but she was not prepared for what was about to happen. Little did she know that within the next few hours, her view of marriage would be changed....*forever!*

The church was small but the interior was immaculate and well decorated. A co-worker had recommended Pastor Lee to them. As they greeted the humble middle-age man that afternoon, they sensed a feeling of trustworthiness.

"Pastor Lee... and you are Allen and Brenda...right?"
They nodded in reply.

As they sat down, Pastor Lee asked for a little more background information about their lives. Brenda and Allen opened up right away. The couple talked back and forth lovingly and with obvious excitement for a few minutes, but they were unprepared for the emotional bomb that the pastor was about to drop. Looking both of them in the eyes, he said, *"I can't marry you!"*

A wave of shock and bewilderment swept over Allen and Brenda faces. This was totally unexpected. Seeing their response, Pastor Lee took his bible and laid it on the desktop and said quietly, *"Please allow me to explain."* Allen sat up looking directly into the pastor's face as he continued to speak. *"If I were to marry you, this would be an injustice to the sanctity of marriage."*

Allen responded quickly, *"Sir, are you serious, what are you talking about?"*

Pastor Lee was silent for a second, then reached across his desk and retrieved his bible. Turning to Matthew chapter 18 to Jesus' teaching on forgiveness, he sought to give the couple a complete understanding to one of mankind's greatest emotional problems, and its consequences. He then turned to Matthew 19 and the Pharisees misunderstanding of this concept.

He showed them how in response to this teaching, the Pharisees in Matthew chapter 19 asked Jesus (paraphrased) *"If we ought to live on this level of forgiveness by not putting away our wives, why did Moses suffer the people to put away their wives and obtain a bill of divorcement"*. Jesus reiterated the depth of unforgiveness when he replied, *"Because of the hardness of your hearts, Moses, suffered (allowed) you to put away your wives: but from the beginning it was not so."*

Allen and Brenda now a bit disgusted, just wanted to leave but felt constrained to finish the counseling session. *"So what has that to do with us, what are you trying to say? Brenda and I have no issues between us!"* Allen said adamantly.

"*Hold your peace*," replied Pastor Lee, "*you came to me for counsel, and I must counsel you according to the word of God.*"

Allen continued on, "*But you already said we can't be married, what's up with this!*"

Pastor Lee continued, "*You can be married if you so desire, but it will not be lawful in the sight of God because of the divorce.*"

Brenda interjected quickly, "*Marriage is lawful, according to my bible, and besides, one can be divorced in the case of adultery.*"

Pastor Lee smiled at Brenda's haste to defend herself before saying, "*That is true, to a point! Marriage is honorable in all, meaning that whether sinner or saint, God will honor one's desire to marry, and the bed is undefiled, but adultery as a cause to sever marital ties is not lawful. God's word states and I quote, 'Except it be for fornication.*"

Brenda's reaction showed clearly on her face, and she rose from her seat with the intention of leaving, but Allen pulled her down as Pastor Lee went on.

After a few seconds of pause, he continued, "*I want to explain to you the exception clause of fornication.*" Turning to Allen he asked, "*You have never been married, am I right?*"

Allen answered, "*Yes you're right, but.....*"

"Hold on," interrupted Pastor Lee, *"your wife-to-be, has been married?"* *"Correct,"* Brenda jumped in.

Pastor Lee continued, *"Should you enter into a marriage relationship, you will commit the sin of fornication by entering into a sexual relationship with this lady. Fornication is sexual relations outside of a lawful marriage covenant. It is not lawful in the sight of God for you to take your neighbor's wife, this is unclean my son! It is uncleanness before the Almighty God!"*

"Hold it Sir!" Allen demanded while jumping to his feet, but this time Brenda quickly pulled him down, as she beckoned to Pastor Lee to continue.

"Brenda on the other hand is married and therefore is unable to commit fornication in this sense, but adultery, because she has a living husband from a biblically lawful marriage.

'And I say unto you, whosoever shall put away his wife, except it be for fornication and shall marry another, committeth adultery; and whosoever marrieth her which is put away doth commit adultery. Matthew 19:9"

"My husband committed fornication!" Brenda declared emphatically.

"Your husband was in a lawful marriage, he committed adultery; there is a difference you know!" Pastor Lee rebutted,

"*Well anyway*," Brenda went on, determined to make her point, "*I'm divorced, and my marriage was ended.*"

"*By whom?*" Pastor Lee asked.

"*By the law of the land,*" Brenda responded in defense.

"*Did the law of the land join you together? Jesus said what he hath joined together let not man put asunder,*" Pastor Lee solemnly answered.

"*Now you're telling me that the law of the land is invalid!*" Brenda rebutted.

"*Let me say this, if and when the law of the land is contrary to the word of God, you cannot obey it. You can read the story of Shadrack, Meshach, and Abednego, along with the story of Daniel in the book of Daniel, or Acts Chapter 5. The law of the land was written to regulate lawless citizens of this world and laws of God are given to regulate citizens of his kingdoms. Of course, God wants us to be good law abiding citizens, however with his servants, God's laws supersede the laws of land.*"

Pastor Lee went on, "*My daughter, let me tell you about divorce. It is not as casual as many may have led you to believe. It is a spiritual death to the institution of marriage, enforced by the spirit of division. Where the spirit of division reigns, you will most likely find mass cases of conflict, offenses, rivalry, intolerance, prejudice, and divorce."*

The couple's eyes grew wide, as the pastor continued, *"You will not only find that spirit in marriages, but in many relationships, mother/daughter, sister/brother, and even among co-workers. Many have separated themselves from the other because of an issue that a hard heart refuses to pardon. Left in the hand of man, this lifeless relationship will always bring destruction, pain, and much confusion, but when our grievances are placed in the hand of God, he can bring that which is considered dead back to life again."*

Brenda could not believe her ears, she had one more thing to say, and then she would be out of this crazy place. Looking the pastor in the eye, she said to him, *"I wasn't a Christian when all that happened, so that does not count!"*

Pastor Lee became passionate. *"You are a Christian now. It is your duty to seek reconciliation at all cost. And besides that, marriage is not only honorable for Christians, in fact, marriage was instituted before Christianity. So when you say that you were not a Christian back then, are you saying that Adam and Eve, Abraham and Sarah, Isaac and Rebecca, all these marriages are void?"*

Brenda and Allen looked horrified as Pastor Lee continued. *"Before you gave your life to Jesus Christ, the word of God did not govern your life. Then, you gave your life to Christ, and immediately the word became your rule of faith, practice, and discipline. In the scriptures that I have read to you tonight, it tells you that your first course of action now is to exercise forgiveness, just as Christ has forgiven you. Unforgiveness brought you to the place that you are today, along with the hardness of your heart to forgive your husband and surrender your broken marriage to the Lord. I want you to know my daughter, that when you reject forgiveness you reject grace to obtain forgiveness for yourself, remember the prayer….and forgive us our debt as we forgive our debtors."*

At that point, Allen spoke up, *"And what about me?"*

"Well my son, yours is a situation of ignorance, you misunderstood the situation that you were getting into and what the word of God said about it. I have counseled many singles like you in an effort to help them avoid situations like this," was Pastor's Lee's quick response.

The counseling session continued, *"I was told that my sins and first marriage was under the blood,"* Brenda said quietly.

"*Your sin is,*" the pastor replied, "*but your marriage is still valid in the sight of God, the only way it can be ended is through death. Until then you cannot enter another marriage relationship or you will be living in the uncleanness of adultery, or for Allen, the sin of fornication. Read it for yourself!*" Pastor Lee placed the bible on top of the desk,

As her trembling fingers followed the words of Matthew 19:9, Brenda read the scripture aloud, **"*And I say unto you, whosoever shall put away his wife, except it be for fornication, and shall marry another, committeth adultery: and whoso marrieth her which is put away doth commit adultery.*"**

Brenda lifted her head to look at Allen, who appeared as if he was about to pass out. Pastor Lee got up to get them both a cup of water, neither said a word as he continued.

"*Now let's say that you were already married, Allen here would be able to divorce you to free himself from fornication, that is the exception clause for the third party in a 'lawful' marriage covenant.*" Pastor Lee could sense the couple's disappointment and tried to console them. "*I can understand how you must feel*," he said to them as he again took his seat. "*Most couples react much like the way you are right now, and so did the disciples, in fact they said to Jesus (Matthews 19:10), If this is the case it is best to never marry, meaning that if marriage is so* binding then it is best not to commit to it. In reply, Jesus told them, *All men cannot accept the life of a Eunuch, though men have chosen this path for many different reasons, to those who can be faithful, let him be.*"

Brenda spoke up, "*I do not want to live alone.*"

With much compassion in his voice, Pastor Lee answered her, "*You don't have to, you have a husband!*"

Brenda's facial expression changed to anger as the tears rolled down her face, "*I divorced him sir, can't you understand, I don't love him anymore That part of my life is finished.*"

Getting up, Pastor Lee handed Brenda a facial tissue, and speaking to her very gently, he asked another question. "*Brenda, whose decision was that, God, or your own? And besides, who is to say that Allen here will not make the same mistake or do something worse?*" From the corner of his eye he saw Allen's defensive reaction, and turned to settle him, "*It's okay my son, let me minister here a while.*" Brenda's sobs grew louder, as Allen moved closer to hold her. For a moment no one spoke.

Barely able to utter her words, Brenda murmured, "*I feel like God has me locked in right about now. It all seems so unfair. I thought He wanted me to be happy.*"

The pastor smiled, *"Yes, God wants you to be happy indeed, but not at the expense of your soul. Remember what you read in I Corinthians 6:9-10, that neither fornicators, nor idolaters, nor adulterers.....shall inherit the kingdom of God. How sad to be happy on this earth, only to be lost eternally and separated from God. It will not be worth it my sister. The root of real happiness is not found in your flesh, but it flows from your spirit and is nourished by a personal relationship with the Lord.*

Pastor Lee sat back in his chair as Brenda spoke again, *"Sir, suppose he was mentally ill and my life was in danger, would I still be locked in this that marriage?"*

"Well Brenda," the Pastor went on to say, *"There are some cases that become life threatening, or emotionally crippling, where a spouse must legally separate himself or herself. Surely if your husband was abusing you and your life was in danger, you must use wisdom and protect your life, However, abuse and other similar problems, no matter how great or small are not a ticket to freedom. Additionally, there is no need to feel locked up because you do have a choice. It may not be what you want, but it is what the Word recommends; if you want to do it God's way, remain single, or resort to getting help for your spouse and get back into the marriage ring and fight! If it is your desire, God can bring life back to your dead marriage."*

And unto the married I command, yet not I, but the Lord,
Let not the wife depart from her husband,
but and if she depart, let her remain unmarried or be reconciled to her husband, and let not the husband
put away his wife. 1 Corinthians 7:10-11.

Pastor Lee paused again, seemingly to allow the young man and woman to absorb what he had just said, before going on. Allen had been sitting quietly until then. *"So are you saying we can't be married,"* he asked?

"That is your decision," the pastor replied, *"But you will be committing the sin of fornication as a single man in relations with a woman outside a lawful marriage covenant."*

Allen shook his head as he leaned forward and took a deep breath. *"This is a mess,"* he finally said.

"It is indeed!" the pastor replied, *"You can follow the circus and do as you please; or you can dance from one relationship to another and yet another Hollywood style. But if you desire a marriage relationship that is built on the principles of God's word and one that can be a foundation for generations, your community, and your nation, you might want to take a second look at what will become the foundation for this marriage."*

"Fornication, fornication...," Allen repeated. *"I never even considered it, and somehow I thought that was only in the case of pre-marital sex."*

"True," replied Pastor Lee, *"and also in this situation, because if you marry her, you would bring yourself into continual sin, in other words, you will resign yourself to fornication or unlawful sex with this married woman. As for Brenda, she will resign herself to the sin of adultery, because as a married woman she would be in a relation outside her lawful marriage covenant."* Allen and Brenda sat back as Pastor Lee said to Allen in a firm voice, *"You need to find your **own** wife; this one already belongs to someone else."*

**Nevertheless, to avoid fornication, let every man have his own wife,
and let every woman have her own husband,
1 Corinthians 7:2.**

Brenda spoke again, *"My first pastor was a man of God and he is married again, are you telling me that he too is living in adultery?"*

"Possibly," Pastor Lee started to say, *"that depends on...."* but before he could finish, Allen interrupted.

"Wait, a minute, depends on what, whether he is wearing a robe or not!"

Pastor Lee shook his head, *"No, no, hold it, be patient, and let me finish. If he is married to another woman while his wife of a lawful marriage is alive, then, yes, he is living in adultery."*

Both Allen and Brenda were amazed, *"But how can this be? Are you sure what you are saying is true; surely I should have heard this before. And besides, there are many great men and women of God that I know who are divorced and remarried."*

"Well my child," replied Pastor Lee in a fatherly tone, *"There is much more that I can show you in confirmation of God's word, if you would allow me. I too am aware of the many men and women of God that are caught in this error, however, I am not here to condemn them, and besides there are unresolved issues in all of our spiritual lives that need to be dealt with, my life included. However just like today, God in his time will present to us the truth, and it is our choice to accept or reject it. When we realize that our life living is not in fellowship with the word of God, we will either submit or rebel."*

For a moment you could hear a pin drop. *"So where do I go from here?"* Brenda asked.

Again, Pastor Lee answered her very solemnly, *"I encourage you, don't just take my word, but go before the Lord in sincerity, and seek his guidance, and He will confirm the truth of His Word."*

This concluded their counseling session. Both Allen and Brenda left with heavy hearts. After dropping Allen off, Brenda took the long way home.

She just wanted to think. In her spirit, she knew what Pastor Lee had said was true. What he said had answered so many of the questions she had asked God secretly.

Most ministers who counseled with her had given her encouragement, but none was as forthright as this man. She thought it would be easy to move away, and go on with her life, but that was not so. She realized that unforgiveness in her heart toward Cameron, coupled with her strong desire to marry Allen were the only things standing in the way of the a reconciliation of her first marriage. Again she began to think back to when she and Cameron had made that covenant with God:

"For better or worse,
For richer or poorer,
In sickness and in health,
We will love and cherish
each other for as long as we both shall live."

Everything was so perfect that day. They didn't envision that marriage would bring problems that would test that promise.

Allen did not call Brenda that night; he didn't know what to say. He had always thought that Cameron brought his misfortune on himself, so he was entitled to rescue this lonely and hurt young woman. But, now he realized that no matter what happened, he was a fifth wheel in this relationship, he had to let it go. As a man of God, his ultimate desire was to live his life in obedience to God's Word.

Brenda, a few miles away was somehow glad that Allen did not call that evening, because she really did not want to talk. On her way home she had stopped by the home of her older sister, and told her of the meeting with Pastor Lee.

Wanting to appease Brenda, her sister was quick to respond, *"Brenda, that is the most ridiculous thing I have ever heard, do not cancel your wedding. That minister does not know what he is saying."*

But in her heart, Brenda knew the Lord had spoken to her. She had often heard these things discussed in religious circles, but she had never come across anyone that was as bold and clear as this pastor. Most people would see it as foolishness, but Brenda knew it was the truth.

When she finally got home, she got something to eat and lay across her bed to think. She couldn't get 1 Corinthians 7:39 out of her head. *"So marriage is until death?"* She said to herself. She realized that she had two choices, either remain unmarried or reconcile with Cameron. Brenda knew that she didn't want to remain alone for the rest of her life. She loved marriage and always desired to have children. Then, there was Cameron, and the issue of his unfaithfulness. Was she willing to help him or even stand by him as he worked through his problem? She reached for her bible and began to thumb through. All of a sudden, her eyes focused on a verse of scripture that spoke directly to her situation. She couldn't believe it. Quickly she sat up and read the passage for herself.

"Then Peter came to him, and said, Lord how oft shall my brother sin against me and I forgive him? Till seven times? Jesus saith unto him, I say not unto thee, until seven times, but until seventy times seven."

At that moment, it felt as if everything changed. Somewhere deep in her heart a barrier was torn down and her tears began to flow. Brenda found herself wailing before the Lord. *"Oh Father, she cried, please forgive me, I did not realize that I was so wrong and so ignorant of your word. Heal my unforgiving heart and show me your perfect will for my life. I need your help in forgiving my husband, I need you to restore this marriage, and I cannot do it by myself."* Brenda knew her prayer was answered when she felt the peace of the Holy Spirit. It was the same peace that was present one year later when she and Cameron renewed their marriage vows.

Tears filled her eyes later as she heard her husband testify of how God had answered his prayer and brought his wife home. *"Now I know how God felt when man fell. He would give anything to bring man back and have their relationship restored."*

Once again she had given her hand to her husband, and they both were overtaken with joy knowing this was indeed the work of the Holy Spirit. Cameron turned to the small crowd of family and friends, *"Now I know that he is truly the God of a second chance, and he has given us a second chance at love."*

Pastor Lee who had disrupted Brenda's life more than twelve months before, pulled the couple to himself and gave them a hug as he quoted 2 Corinthians 5:18, *"All things are of God who had reconciled us to himself by Jesus Christ, and hath given to us the ministry of reconciliation!"*

The ministry of reconciliation is that of reuniting man to God and to each other. God sent his only son to die a cruel death on Calvary's cross to reconcile sinful man back to himself. This is the epitome of reconciliation. We must learn and embrace this example, if we want to be in relationship with him. Divorce spurred by unforgiveness, fights to destroy this ministry and message.

2.
Questions Answered

Pastor Winn rushed into his office just in time to begin the meeting with area ministers from his community. Their quarterly meeting was always a good time of conversation, fellowship, and food. Ninety minutes later, the meeting was ended with a word of prayer as the men gathered in the fellowship hall to have a bite to eat together.

"That was a large crowd at noonday prayer yesterday at Pastor Lee's church" one pastor commented.

Pastor Winn chuckled, *"That was no prayer meeting; it was a wedding!"*

"A wedding!" The pastor responded in a surprised tone. *"In the middle of the week, couldn't they wait until Saturday?"*

"No they couldn't, they had waited long enough." Pastor Winn replied. *"Actually, that particular couple was divorced for almost two years! They reconciled and recommitted."*

"That's confusion," another pastor spoke up, **"didn't the bible say that once you have left your spouse you should not return."**

"No, it didn't," Pastor Winn said firmly. **"Many people have misinterpreted God's word, but**

we as ministers must know the truth in order that we can lead God's people.

"*Well what did it say?*" Elder Rushmore asked sarcastically?

"*Let me explain this,*" Pastor Winn went on as more of the ministers drew near as he whipped out his pocket bible and began to read a passage from scripture. "*What you are talking about is found right here in the book of Jeremiah...*"

"***They say, If a man put away his wife, and she go from him, and become another man's, shall he return unto her again? Shall not that land be greatly polluted? But thou hast played the harlot with many lovers, yet returned again to me, saith the Lord. Jeremiah 3:1***"

Pastor Winn continued, "*I was told the same thing years ago in seminary, but it wasn't until years later that I discovered the truth. The question was answered by God himself who validated that if a man could not forgive his wife, then how could he expect forgiveness from God. It was a response to a backsliding nation. Using the relationship of the man who had walked away from his wife, he explained that if it were true that the woman could not come back to the husband because it would be wrong, how is it right for those that were backslidden to return unto him. When you understand marriage, then, you can understand the relationship of Christ and his*

Church, and to understand that is to understand what was being said in that passage."

Turning to another passage of scripture, Pastor Winn reinforced his point. *"You see, the Lord always hated divorce, and stated so in Malachi 2:14 through 16, it says, 'Yet ye say, Wherefore? Because the LORD hath been witness between thee and the wife of thy youth, against whom thou hast dealt treacherously: yet is she thy companion, and the wife of thy covenant. And did not he make one? Yet had he the residue of the spirit. And wherefore one? That he might seek a godly seed. Therefore take heed to your spirit, and let none deal treacherously against the wife of his youth. For the LORD, the God of Israel, saith that he hateth putting away: for one covereth violence with his garment, saith the LORD of hosts: therefore take heed to your spirit, that ye deal not treacherously."*

Pastor Gray interrupted him, *"Well, why was it that David didn't get his wife Michal back if this was so."*

"What are you talking about my brother?" Pastor Winn quickly rebutted. *"I hope you haven't been preaching that,"* he continued as he laughed softly, *"because Michal was returned to her husband. David's wife was taken from him in 1 Samuel 25:44, when Saul gave her, his daughter, to Phalti the son of Laish, which was of Gallim.' And, she was returned to him in 2 Samuel 3:14-16. 'And*

David sent messengers to Ish-bosheth Saul's son, saying, Deliver me my wife: Michal, which I espoused to me for an hundred foreskins of the Philistines. And Ish-bosheth sent, and took her from her husband, even from Phaltiel the son of Laish. And her husband went with her along weeping behind her to Bahurim. Then said Abner unto him, Go, return. And he returned.'

This was done because, Saul, her father, in revenge had given her to another to marry. My brother, the truths concerning marriage is such an awesome message in the body of Christ, because it is the message of the body of Christ and the Lord himself. People are being spiritually destroyed because they do not understand the scriptures. There are many that are married today and their marriages are not lawful in the sight of God."

"What do you mean?" Elder Rushmore asked.

Pastor Winn responded, "*What I am saying is that God does not recognize their union.*"

"How can that be?" Another pastor questioned.

Pastor Winn took a deep breath, "*It is possible to be given a marriage license by the law of a land, go through with a ceremony, repeat the vows, and still not be married.*" When the pastors began to look at him as if he was losing it, Pastor Winn spoke about something that most of them agreed with. "*For example,*" he said, "*Much is being said today about the "gay" marriage, am I right?*"

"*Yes*," a few ministers replied as they turned again to him.

"*I watch them marching and demanding that they be wedded and I know that these people do not even know what marriage is, they have no clue. No matter how many states give them permission to marry, that marriage is not lawful in the sight of God. It is a faulty union, in other words it cannot stick, no glue, it you know what I mean.*" The ministers laughed, they agreed with that. Pastor Winn went on, "*But it goes beyond "gay" marriages, to marriages of multiple partners. How can you ask God to join you to another man's wife or another woman's husband when he clearly states in Leviticus and the gospels that it is sexual uncleanness!*" The room went quiet again.

"*If I preach that in my church, I might as well resign!*" Pastor Ray exclaimed.

"*Resign?*" Another pastor interjected, "*If I were to preach that message in my church, seventy percent of my congregation will walk out.*"

"*Oh I have lost a few*," Pastor Winn added, "*but I have also gained many who desire to know the truth and live by it. That is the fear the enemy uses against us to keep us from preaching a pure gospel. One of the reasons our people are so sick is because their spiritual food is corrupted. Nothing is pure anymore, to the point that the world thinks that even

Christianity is polluted. I believe if we preach and teach people the truth about marriage and the covenant, they will realize that when the issues of life arise in their marriage, divorce is not an option. But hey, marry them if you want, all you are doing is complicating their lives. I only marry singles or widows because that is who my bible tells me are eligible to marry!"

"But how do you know that what you have shared is true, where did you get this from?" The Methodist minister asked.

"I read my bible and the Holy Spirit gives me understanding." Pastor Winn said with a mischievous smile.

"And we don't," the Methodist minister responded.

Pastor Winn smiled, "No, I don't mean that, but of a truth, I received this revelation from the Lord. There was a time that I too feared the truth, until it came into my home. When my son got married, I watched as his family grew. The young woman he married was accepted into our family as our own daughter. When my son came and told my wife and me that he had filed for a divorce, I was devastated. How could I let my daughter go, she had become a part of us, our son, our grandkids, our family. I tried to accept it at first, but I couldn't. I talked to my son, but his mind was made up. In fact he was seeing another young woman in our church.

I was praying in my study one afternoon and I saw the spirit of division stand up tall in the foyer of my home. It was a hideous creature. At that moment, I cried out to God and it disappeared, but God was showing me that my home was under attack by the spirit of division. I went on an immediate fast for my son and daughter-in-law and God came through for me. God restored their marriage, and this is when he unveiled the truth about divorce and remarriage to me. I now vow to tell others that the fight for your marriage is much more spiritual than physical."

"Yes," Elder Rawlins added, *"but not every marriage will last, and in some cases it is better to get out of a marriage."*

The Pentecostal Pastor spoke up, *"That is easier said than done for many people. What you do not realize is the marriage is a bond of soul and spirit; it is easy to get into but hard to get out. That's why it is called a lifetime commitment."*

"That's right!" Pastor Winn agreed, *"And only God himself can declare a marriage and only he can truly take you out. That's a fact. One thing is true when it comes to a lawful marriage it is like egg, it cannot be unscrambled. Once God joins two people together, that is a lifetime commitment that cannot be broken by mankind."*

The Baptist Pastor came and sat down at the table, but before he began to eat, he had a question, *"So you are trying to tell me that if a woman in my church is being abused by her husband, I should tell her that marriage is a lifetime commitment, and there is no way out?"*

Pastor Winn chuckled, *"Come on now, this is why you are a minister, you counsel to the whole man."* Turning to address the group of men, he continued, *"Abuse in any form is grievous indeed, it would anger any of us to see someone being physically taken advantage of in a relationship. The first thing that must be done in any abusive situation is to consult the Holy Spirit for direction and instructions. He has firsthand information concerning every situation. You should also call on a few mature but prayerful saints to cover you, and the family in prayer so that God's will prevails. Then sit down with the individuals involved to uncover the root situation. It could be an issue with the husband, or wife. The next step is to begin working with each individual to work through or resolve the underlying issue. There are some cases where you as a pastor might have to separate the couple by finding lodging for either one for a few weeks sometimes months while you work with the family".*

"That could be a lot of work, and it sounds expensive," the minister from the Lutheran church acknowledged.

"Well maintaining marriage and family is a lot of work, and ministry always calls for money, but these are the areas that our money needs to be applied to, the tangible workings of building lives." Pastor Winn stated, *"Trust me, if you take care of the people and put their needs first, money will come to take care of the religious toys. Marriage and family are the very foundation of your ministry."*

Pastor Valtos spoke, *"What if you do all of that and you still can't help them, then we are still back to the divorce court? I remember counseling a wife whose husband abandoned the marriage; I felt peace in telling her she was free to divorce and remarry according to Paul's teaching in 1 Corinthians 7:15 that says a brother or sister is not under bondage in such cases."*

Pastor Winn was quiet for a moment before he answered. *"You know my mother went through that same scenario. My father abandoned the marriage for another woman leaving her to care for us alone. As a little boy, I thought the whole world had come to an end."* Tears came to his eyes as he continued.

"But God...but God! With the support of her church, and family members, we weathered the storm. My mother became a tower of strength in faith as we proved God in paying our bills and keeping us boys out of trouble...it was four of us!

It's amazing how we use scriptures to bail us out of carrying a cross. Brother Valtos, our crosses were not meant to destroy us, they were meant to build faith and character as we learn to trust God in the most trying circumstances. And, besides, in that scripture, Paul was simply saying that if a husband or wife left, a brother or sister was no longer burdened or obligated to keep the duties of marriage.

Doesn't the Apostle Paul after saying a brother or sister is not in bondage in such cases say, 'For what knowest thou, O wife, whether thou shalt save thy husband? or how knowest thou, O man, whether thou shalt save thy wife?' Meaning we should continually strive whether in prayers or our life living to bring the other spouse to Christ.

Divorce is never an option, in fact, it is a hell trap where we circumvent faith and Christian virtue to meet our immediate needs." Pastor Winn stopped before saying some solemn words. "My brothers, we have compromised enough, and our compromising has put a lot of people into a very bad spiritual position."

These words seemed to bite deeply, and even the pastor from the Christian church who had been enjoying his meal quietly, felt obligated to question Pastor Winn's judgment. "So you believe that divorce cannot be forgiven, it is not the unpardonable sin you know."

"Of course it is not the unpardonable sin, but it will lead to an individual turning his back on receiving pardon," said Pastor Winn. *"Jesus said, If you do not forgive others, then neither can I forgive you."*

"I hear what you are saying brother Winn, but I do not believe that a loving God would send someone to hell just because they want to be married!" Bishop Norman added.

Pastor Winn quickly responded, *"This is something I hear often as I counsel couples. It is confusing when we don't know how to rightly divide scripture. Because truly God is a loving God, and no he will never send someone to hell just because they want to be married, but if being married becomes sin, our loving God said that he would do so, and swiftly. Remember, the wages of sin is still death."*

The quiet Reverend in the corner said nothing until now, *"People want the pleasure of sin, but avoid the punishment that comes with the package."*
"That is so true," Pastor Winn went on, *"when the Bible clearly tells us that committing adultery or living in a state of adultery is sin"*
"But you have someone who will say, But this makes me happy, surely God wants me to be happy," The Reverend spoke again.

Pastor Winn smiled, because this minister was a man of few words. *"I have also had individuals that came to me and with sincerity say, God told me to divorce my lawful spouse and marry this person,* he added. *I am then put in the position where I have to look them in the eye and say madam or sir you have been deceived by the father of lies because God will never tell you to disobey his word. Now there are some situations where I agree with them."*

"Really?" Elder Rawlins questioned shockingly.

This caused the other ministers to break into laughter. Pastor Winn smiled and continued, *"Yes, there was a young woman who had married a gentleman who had been married twice before. She was his third wife, he was her first husband. The marriage lasted a little more than a year, and she moved out. No doubt her husband was livid and took her to see their pastor, who then referred them to me. When I counseled them, she told me that God told her during a fast to walk away from the marriage. After much thought, she did, and immediately felt peace. I was able to explain the word to both of them and continued to counsel both for a few months thereafter, but it was a difficult situation. My wife assisted me in helping this young woman to get through and move on with her life. At the same time I began to work with the ex-husband in working through his situation and acknowledging the fact that he was still in a lawful marriage to his first wife."*

"Man," Pastor Valtos, the Assembly of God minister said, *"that is confusion if I have ever heard i. It would be easier to just let them continue on and commit to the present relationship."*

"And live in adultery? You really think it is better to continue in sin, that grace might abound?" Pastor Winn passionately interjected!

Again Pastor Valtos spoke, *"But what you are saying gives them no hope, we have to give people hope! Telling them that they cannot be married again and have a second chance at love will break their hearts. There are many that I know of, and even in my church, that will not accept this."*

All was quiet for a moment. Slowly, Pastor Winn raised his head, *"My brothers, must Jesus bear the cross alone and all the world go free? No, there is a cross for all of us, even me. I know this is a hard message to preach and an even harder one to swallow, but it is a cross that many will have to bear. When God told Cain of the consequences that would follow him as a result of him actions (Genesis 4:11-13) he said, 'My punishment is more than I can bear.'"*

Elder Rawlins then said, *"But that was a result of a curse upon him, remarriage is not a curse."*

Pastor Winn was quick to reply, *"Not so fast Elder, the consequences of disobedience awakens the* curse of sin. To walk away from a biblically lawful marriage and marry another while your spouse is alive is adultery according to the Word of God, which is sin that leads to spiritual death. It is as simple as that. We must teach God's people the necessity of living by faith, taking up their crosses, and bringing their lives in obedience to him."

"I don't know about this," Pastor Valtos said again, "I have to study this and pray about this, because somehow it seems too much to ask. Like the brother said, a teaching like that will destroy my church; I have never heard it explained like that before. I also need to speak to my Superintendent to find out exactly how our denomination views this, because didn't Paul say in Corinthians that....."

Before Pastor Valtos could continue, Pastor Winn interjected, "My brother, if you read Paul's teaching carefully, you will see that Paul was not preaching something new, he was simply validating what Jesus said in Matthew 19, that marriage is a binding agreement between God and man. But like I always tell you brothers, do not take my word for gospel, get on your faces before God and let him give you his answers. That's the correct thing to do Brother Valtos."

Pastor Winn continued as he turned to the pastors, "Pray and ask God to give you revelation and understanding. Then, you will be able to preach with conviction and with the wisdom of God. I know this message might sound strange because few, even among us, are willing to preach the biblical view of marriage, which is why the divorce rate in the church is surpassing that of unbelievers. But it is all there in the word of God. It is not our place to judge it, only to preach and declare it."

Reverend Brown stood up to get another piece of cake, but not before saying, "*That is why I do not get deep into marital counseling, after a while it gets too complicated, I let them do what they want to do because I have neither the time or patience to deal with that.*"

"*But this is all a part of being a minister*," the Pentecostal pastor commented, "*this is what you said you are called to do, lead God's people according to his word, and besides you have a responsibility. When we try to lead people according to what we believe, you are right, it becomes overwhelming. When you are at your ropes end, God is always there to help you, because you did not choose him, he chose you.*"

Pastor Meyers, the minister at the Baptist church in the heart of the city, was silent until then. Finally, he responded, "*This is why marriage is the way it is today. I have been pastoring the oldest Baptist church in the city for twenty-one years and this is the first time I have really gotten an *understanding of the mess that marriages are in. They come in to see me all the time and I too am frustrated by the issues. It has caused me to take the easy way out, but how many homes and lives have I mislead over the years. I feel sick."*

"*Do you realize that this was the reason why John the Baptist was beheaded?*" (Mark 6:16-28) Pastor Winn asked him before going on to explain, "*Herod was committing adultery by being married to Herodias, his brother Philip's wife. She got into an argument with John because she did not want to hear that they were living in sin. So they axed him. Many times today, I feel that if people could axe me for standing on what the word said about marriage, they would.*"

"*What do we do, where do we go from here?*" Elder Rawlins asked solemnly.
"*Preach the word, tell the people the truth and let the chips fall where they may!*" Pastor Winn said firmly. "*The word is a two-edged sword that cuts, but it also heals. The truth will anger some, but it will liberate many! And keep in mind the word spoken in Luke 18:27 which says, 'The things which are impossible with men are possible with God.*"

Before long the meeting came to an end as the evening drew near. Minister Marvin, one of the youngest pastors in attendance, was the first to ask to be excused. As he walked away, his heart was so heavy in his chest, he contemplated stopping at his doctor's office before heading home. He knew how Pastor Winn felt about divorce and remarriage, but had always brushed past him quickly, but today Pastor Winn's word hit home.

His mind went back to his first marriage. His wife Collette was the prettiest and most attractive girl in the choir, but more than that she loved the Lord with all her heart. They didn't have a long courtship and were married soon after he graduated from seminary. Shortly after, they started a church and it grew quickly. As a couple, they were happy and began their family, but after the second baby it was hard not notice how much heavier his wife hat gotten. He tried over and over to get her into a weight-loss program at the gym, but she always had an excuse.

The marriage began to sour as day after day every small comment became a major event of fussing and harsh words. Each began to pull away from the other. It wasn't long after the couple separated that Marvin fell in love with Keisha McNeil. Keisha was fresh out of college and had a very shapely body. Within months, Collette was out and Keisha was the new First Lady.

This affected the church greatly. Keisha occupied much more of his time so his secretary wrote his sermons. Church attendance and the offering were reduced tremendously. But after a few months, the congregation began to grow again and things slowly returned to normal. However, Marvin felt guilty about the quick divorce, and the guilt caused him many sleepless nights.

The scripture about dealing treacherously with the wife of one's youth kept coming to his mind but he always brushed it aside. (Malachi 2:15) He blamed Collette's weight problem for the marriage ending. But what could he do, he reasoned. Surely, God wanted him to be happy, and he was happy with his new young wife. Nevertheless, today he was brought back to reality as the Pastor Winn's words cut deep into his soul and spirit. *"If what the pastor said was not true, he reasoned within himself, why was he so convicted?"* As his car came to a stop in the parking lot of his church, he hung his head and with tears in his eyes whispered, *"Dear God, please help me!"*

His mind went back to last week when Collette came to pick up the children. It hurt to see the pain in her eyes. He knew he had scarred her deeply. She had trimmed down a whole lot and looked great. So good in fact that he had come close to pulling her to himself and kissing her, but the children came into the kitchen before he could act on his emotions. He knew it was a good thing that Keisha was not home.

From that day, he kept wondering how he could have made such a big mistake. Keisha was a good wife, but Collette had been a good wife and a true minister's companion. It didn't help that she was now attending the Pentecostal church on the other street and making waves in that ministry. Minister Marvin burst into tears; he knew that the problem was not with his marriage or his wives, but with his own heart. Instantly, the scriptures in Mark 7:18-22 filled his mind.

> *"And he said, That which cometh out of the man, that defileth the man. For from within, out of the heart of man proceed evil thoughts, adulteries, fornications, murders, thefts, covetousness, wickedness, deceit, lasciviousness, an evil eye, blasphemy, pride, foolishness, all these evil things come from within, and defile the man. Mark 7:20-23"*

He knew what he had to do. Rushing into his office, he picked up the telephone and dialed a number he never thought that he would.

The gentle voice on the other end said, *"Hello, may I help."*

Hardly able to speak as his voice cracked, *"Good afternoon, Ms. Hall, this is Minister Marvin Simms, I need to make an appointment to speak with Pastor Winn!"*

3.
Grace, Grace, God's Grace!

The purpose of this book is not condemnation. The Lord did not come into the world to condemn people for their sins. He came to save and deliver. However, I believe that the truth of marriage, divorce and remarriage has always been controversial because it deals with some of our most basic and fundamental human needs of companionship and sexual fulfillment.

When we are faced with being deprived of these needs, most of us make drastic decisions to either protect ourselves or ensure our further access to these needs. Without genuine faith and a clear understanding of marriage, we take matters into our own hands, making a bad situation worse.

Indeed, no one gets married to be divorced in a few months. We dream of the happily ever after, and fulfillment of our passions and desires. Most of us never envision the tremendous fight that comes to destroy the marriage relationship. Alas, and sadly, during our time, most of our dreams and desires end with separation and divorce.

Divorce, once taboo in earlier times is now commonplace. A young divorced woman who appeared on one of our Marriage Mechanics TV Programs made the comment, *"I would not wish divorce on my worst enemies."* She recounted the pain, shame, and emotional rape that she had endured and stated emphatically, *"never again."* A friend, who is divorced, said, *"I thought divorce was going to be a one, two, three situation between my ex-wife and me. I thought because we were mature people, our divorce would be easy. What a laugh! We went through hell!"*

Divorce is never easy, especially for two people who had planned to spend the rest of their lives together. The custody battles, the visitation rights, alimony, asset sharing, name changes, all wreak havoc on the splitting couple. Only those who have experienced divorce know of the pain and scars it leaves behind. Divorce was never God's plan and those who choose to embrace it, or are victims of divorce are never the same afterward.

But the reality and truth behind many divorces is ignorance, immaturity, bigotry and in some cases rebellion against the word of God. There are some people who are not aware of the unadulterated truth about divorce, others need encouragement to get back on the right side of the track, and still some need a sharp word of rebuke for their rebellious behavior to help them avoid a painful decision and eventual condemnation from the Lord.

Mat 19:3-10 "The Pharisees also came unto him, tempting him, and saying unto him, Is it lawful for a man to put away his wife for every cause? And he answered and said unto them, Have ye not read, that he which made them at the beginning made them male and female, And said, For this cause shall a man leave father and mother, and shall cleave to his wife: and they twain shall be one flesh Wherefore they are no more twain, but one flesh. What therefore God hath joined together, let not man put asunder. They say unto him, Why did Moses then command to give a writing of divorcement, and to put her away He saith unto them, Moses because of the hardness of your hearts suffered you to put away your wives: but from the beginning it was not so. And I say unto you, whosoever shall put away his wife, except it be for fornication, and shall marry another, committeth adultery: and whoso marrieth her which is put away doth commit adultery. His disciples say unto him, If the case of the man be so with his wife, it is not good to marry."

The word divorce is explained today as legally dissolving a marriage or as the Greek word for divorcement in Matthew 19 infers **severance** of married partners. Over the years, Satan and his cohorts of demons have covered up, and purposely misconstrued the truth about divorce. His desire is to produce a generation of selfish, self-centered individuals who are fearful and afraid of commitment. You see, hurt people are usually very insecure, and cannot form viable relationships because the pain of rejection and unforgiveness inhibits their ability to trust again. Most simply take care of themselves and resort to manipulation, fear, or control to keep relationships going.

Without prayer and a humble desire for the truth, most theologians and church leaders miss the opportunity to inspire individuals, strengthen families, restore communities, and build nations. Looking at divorce from purely a doctrinal point of view, they fall into the satanic trap of validating divorce. Like the Pharisees of old, they still approach divorce from a human point of view. *"Is it lawful for a man to put away his wife for **every cause?**"* (Matthew 19:3) Or, in layman's language, *"Doesn't certain circumstances permit divorce?"*

Like the Pharisees, the misunderstanding of marriage and why people get divorced is still the same. Our human pride and arrogance blind us to the deeper truths of God. **Divorce is perpetrated by a**

condition of the heart - an unforgiving heart. It is a heart not head matter. With divorce we are dealing with a *motive* rather than *information*. A motive is a root cause while information means we are dealing with circumstances as we see them: human reasoning, while rationalizing circumstances, which usually lead us further away from the truth.

For example, Sheila marries John. Sheila is committed to her marriage. John, on the other hand initially felt that he was in love with Sheila, after a few years of marriage feels he needs a new romance. This leads him outside of his relationship and into the arms of another woman. To the human's mind, this is justified grounds for divorce. Sheila has been wronged. She has the right to cut off the offending party and remarry if she chooses. However, the answer to hurt is not to hurt back; we only continue the pain if we do. Also, we become like the people who we are trying to cut off by falling into the satanic trap of unforgiveness and rejection. In other words, **we become the people we hate**. There is only one way, and only **one way**, to overcome "evil" and that is with "good." *Romans 12:21, "Be not overcome of evil, but overcome evil with good."*

The **unforgiving heart** is usually at the root of most divorces. Instead of going to God for wisdom and healing, people take matters into their own hands. When we understand this, then we can look at the broader spectrum of divorce from a biblical point of view. Like Jesus said, *"...in the beginning it was not so."* We must remember, divorce was never God's original plan and the marriage covenant is like the covenant that God made with his people: unalterable. *"Turn, O backsliding children saith the Lord; for I am married unto you; and I will take you one of a city, and two of a family, and I will bring you to Zion."* **(Jeremiah 50:5)**

The book of Ecclesiastes warns people about the seriousness of making vows. *"When thou vowest a vow unto God, defer not to pay it for he hath no pleasure in fools pay that which thou hast vowed. <u>Better is it that thou shouldest not vow than that thou shouldest vow and not pay.</u> Suffer not thy mouth to cause thy flesh to sin neither say thou before the angel, that it was an error: wherefore should God be angry at thy voice and destroy the work of thy hands?" (Ecclesiastes 5:4-6)*

When Jesus answered the Pharisees' question in Matthew 19, he first dealt with what made a man and woman, husband and wife. When a man and woman get married, <u>God's spiritual law goes into effect</u> *"Therefore shall **a man** leave his father and his mother and shall cleave unto his wife: **and they shall be one flesh.**" Genesis 2:24 "Wherefore they are **no more twain, but one flesh**. What therefore **God hath joined together**, let not man put asunder."* The ***one flesh*** is what most people miss. A husband and wife become one flesh, **joined supernaturally** by God himself. Whether they got married in a disco or parachuting ten thousand feet to the ground, once they have taken their vows and made a covenant with each other and God, within the right parameters, i.e. everyone in his right mind and understand what they are doing, and free and lawful agents for marriage, they become one flesh, case closed!

Of course, this was not enough to convince our studious religious leaders, and they were quick to answer Jesus that Moses authorized divorce. They rehearsed *Deuteronomy 24:1* *"When a man hath taken a wife, and married her, and it come to pass that she find no favor in his eyes, because he hath found some uncleanness in her then let him write her a bill of divorcement, and give it in her hand, and send her out of his house."* However, Jesus reminded the Pharisees that this clause under the law, was never God's perfect will. **Moses amendment <u>24:1 section *Deuteronomy*</u>**, was always in contradiction and violation of section *2:24 Genesis*, and was only a ***temporary reprieve*** (allowance) added to appease **hard-hearted people (unforgiving, insensitive and wounded people)** and furthermore *24:1 **was now invalid***. Why? **Grace** is now available through the blood of Jesus Christ and His limitless power.

Others, using Matthew 19:9 and Matthew 5:32 as ammunition-the only verses in the gospels to have some semblance of condoning divorce-claim that their mates committed adultery so that gives them the right to divorce. Matthew 19:9 and Matthew 5:32 are precarious (dangerous) passages of scripture to translate and interpret if one's theology is wrong regarding the sanctity of marriage. In fact, and alarmingly, some modern translations have translated this portion of scripture incorrectly! The word ***adultery*** is now being inserted for the word ***fornication*** in some new translations. Could this be another reason why many are resorting to divorce? Indeed, because of this misrepresentation and unprayerful rendering of God's word, these bibles should cease being used in the church at large! *"Every word of God is pure; he is a shield unto them that put their trust in him. Add thou not unto his words, lest he reprove thee, and thou be found a liar." Proverbs 30:5-6*

Jesus states in Matthew 19:9 the only reason a person can remarry: *"And I say unto you, Whoever shall put away his wife, <u>**except**</u> it be for **fornication** (translated from the Greek word porneia) and shall marry another committed **adultery**. (translated from the Greek word moichao): and whoso marrieth her which is put away doth commit adultery."* The Greek word ***porneia*** is usually used in the New Testament to describe all types of sexual immorality, i.e. harlotry, whoredom, but it is contrasted in this passage with ***moichao***, which accurately describes a person who has broken their marriage covenant. The Jews knew exactly what Jesus was talking about as he explained it to them; there was no confusion.

They understood that when Jesus was referring to sexual uncleanness or unlawful sex, he was referring to the law in Leviticus 18:6-20 and Leviticus 20:10-21, which clearly explains sexual immorality.

As indicated in the law, it was sexually wrong to sleep with: one's father; one's mother; one's father's wife; one's granddaughter; one's sister or stepsister; one's aunt; one's daughter-in-law; a mother and her daughter; a mother and her granddaughter; a women and her sister; and/or one's neighbor's wife. If your sexual relationship with your spouse falls under any of these circumstances, you are qualified to get a divorce. In this verse, Jesus was not talking about married persons having illicit affairs. He was simply stating that if husband and wife had a sexually impure or immoral relationship, they could get a divorce. He was never suggesting that since adultery was such a grievous sin that the offended partner could get a divorce. This would have undermined his whole ministry in which he taught forgiveness and reconciliation.

A good illustration of this teaching is when John the Baptist rebuked Herod the tetrarch for marrying his brother Philip's wife because it was unlawful. *"For Herod himself had sent forth and laid hold upon John, and bound him in prison for Herodias sake, his brother Philip's wife: for he had married her. For John had said unto Herod.* ***It is not lawful for thee to have thy brother's' wife****."*

(Mark 6:17-18) Unlawful according to what? According to Leviticus 18:16. John was telling Herod that he should dissolve this illegal marriage because it violated God's laws on sexual morality.

Understanding God's Grace

> *"By whom also we have access by faith into this grace wherein we stand, and rejoice in hope of the glory of God. Romans 5:2"*

> *"Therefore it is of faith, that it might be by grace; to the end the promise might be sure to all the seed; not to that only which is of the law, but to that also which is of the faith of Abraham; who is the father of us all, Roman 4:16"*

Divorce was and never is the answer. Grace is indeed God's unequivocal answer for life's problems. When Jesus Christ died and rose again to sit on the right hand of God, he said these words, *"All power is given unto me in heaven and in earth. Matthew 28:18"* It takes faith, and sometimes a lifetime to comprehend those words, and to understand that whatever happens in my life whether good or bad, God allows it. He is in total control!

Instead of taking our problems to the God *who allowed it* so that he can demonstrate his awesome wisdom and power, we take matters into our foolish hands and make things worse. Then, we wallow in self-pity and strike out in anger, oblivious to our spiritual environment, and ignorant of the grace of God. But what is grace and how can I get it?

Some people use the word grace as an acronym meaning "**G**od's **R**iches **A**t **C**hrist's **E**xpense. Others say that grace is the undeniable power and wisdom of God that cannot be overcome or withstood. Suffice it to say that grace is whatever you need to be victorious in life. It was Paul's answer to a seemingly incurable ailment. *"And he said unto me, My grace is sufficient for thee: for my strength is made perfect in weakness. Most gladly therefore will I rather glory in my infirmities, that the power of Christ may rest upon me. 2 Corinthians 12:9"*

It's Jesus walking on water to meet his disciples. It's the miracle of feeding five thousand with only five loaves and two fishes. It's healing, a vision, and a timely word from the Holy Spirit. It all falls under his grace. In other words, it's his supernatural power coming to the aid of an individual. And, how do they get it? One word: humility. We must submit our circumstances and heart to God. *"But he giveth more grace. Wherefore he saith, God resisteth the proud, but giveth grace unto the humble."* (James 4:6) *"The LORD is nigh unto them that are of a broken heart; and saveth such as be of a contrite spirit." (Psalm 34:18)* "Blessed are the poor in spirit; for theirs is the kingdom of God." *(Matthew 5:1)*

Grace comes as we humble ourselves before the Lord and allow Him to do the work in us and through us. We must put self to rest and take up our crosses and follow him. Therein lies the dilemma of our day. No one wants to suffer. No one wants to be defrauded. No one wants to take the lower position. We want to be always on the top. So we disqualify ourselves from the grace of God.

Indeed, it is not easy to rely on the Lord, especially when all hell is breaking loose around you. We want things to be fixed fast, and in our way. But, grace says, *"Let go and let God."* In fact, without God's grace it's impossible to stay in a problem-filled marriage. Problems come in many shapes and forms: abuse; a marriage where a wife may be adulterous; finding out that one husband committed incest; financial woes, jail, alcohol and the list can go on.

You see, every situation is different and the only way to know how to correctly handle each one is to first seek the direction of God, and act in accordance with his word. We need the grace of his wisdom. There are times when God directs you to stay, but you want to move. Other times he desires you to move, but you desire to stay put.

Because God cannot make mistakes, we can never go wrong when we step forth in faith, take him at his word, and walk in his will. Someone once said, *"He might not come when we want him, but he will always be there on time."* God never promised us life without tribulation, however, he did tell us, *"in your patience possess ye your soul."* We must learn to wait on the Lord until he answers our prayers. *"Wait on the Lord: and be of good courage, and he will strengthen your heart: wait, I say on the Lord."* (Psalm 27:14)

Of course, grace does not mean that if we are in an abusive relationship we should stay in the relationship until we are physically scarred or beaten to death or if we are in an adulterous relationship, we should allow our spouse's lover to move in. The disciples who were persecuted in one city usually escaped to another city.

If the abuse is consistent or repeated, there may be a need to seek a safe haven and seek counseling, but continue to pray and take authority over the spirits that have taken your mate captive. If the adulterous affair continues unabated there may be a good reason to bring the marriage to a crisis, making the offending party choose whom he or she wants have a sexual relationship with by separating. Also, there may a fear of contracting AIDS. (In this case, it may be necessary for the adulterous party to be tested before engaging in sexual relations with a faithful partner) However, during this time of separation, Godly counsel should be sought that may bring reconciliation and foster personal spiritual virtue. This is what Paul is referring to in Corinthians 7:10-11, *"And unto the married I command, yet not I, but the Lord, Let not the wife depart from her husband. But and if she depart, let her remain unmarried, or be reconciled to her husband and let not the husband put away his wife."*

If you are divorced and have sought reconciliation without any success, don't give up! God understands your dilemma. Even if the person remarries, God can still do the impossible. There are times we must wait on God. Those who remarry do so in violation of God's word. 1 Corinthians 7:39 *"The wife is bound by the law as long as her husband liveth, but if her husband be dead, she is at liberty to be married to whom she will, only in the Lord."* Romans 7:2-3, *"For the woman which hath an husband is bound by the law to her husband so long as he liveth; but if the husband be dead, she is loosed from the law of her husband. So then if, while her husband liveth, she be married to another man, she shall be called an adulteress, but if her husband be dead (the widow), she is no adulteress, though she be married to another man."*

Usually, when people get divorced, they find themselves looking for another love relationship. Seeking another husband or wife further compounds the situation. Many people say, *"What am I supposed to do? I have physical needs. I need companionship and sexual fulfillment."* But in times like these, we need to prove God's grace and power. Let God become your lover. Let God fill that void in your life. We expect teenagers and young people to control their sexual appetite, but adults also have the same responsibility. The problem rests in our inner psyche, where the Devil has used the media to create in modern man an insatiable carnal desire. Sex and more sex is the answer to life's problem is the Devil's constant ad campaign. But the Devil is a liar! The answer to your separation or divorce is the infilling presence of the Holy Spirit, our comforter, restorer, healer and counselor.

In the same vein, several years ago, the Holy Spirit spoke to my heart and said, *"Unforgiveness is the rejection of grace."* How powerful and potent were these few words. Indeed, grace comes to us as we weather the storms of life through his comfort and wisdom. He is the one that allows every trial so that we would turn to Him. When we take matters into our own hands, we fall deeper and deeper into the satanic web of unforgiveness and bitterness. When we submit to God the Devil, flees from us as we gain supernatural power to endure our circumstances. The cross is still the way to spiritual maturity; suffering still the way to rule with Christ. *"Submit yourselves therefore to God. Resist the devil, and he will flee from you." (James 4:7)*

Some people after reading this book will say, *"Yeah, what you're saying may be true, but I know some powerful and influential men of God and some anointed women who have remarried."* And yes, God loves them and our attitude toward those who have chosen this route should always be love, compassion and outstretched arms. But, remember Judas was used by God to perform miracles and to be an Apostle, but he had money problems that eventually led to his spiritual demise.

God used Peter awesomely through miracles, signs and wonders, but the Apostle Paul rebuked him for his racial prejudice. The Corinthian Church although plagued with sexual immorality had seemingly had the greatest manifestation of spiritual gifts. Again, the wisest man that ever lived, Solomon, disobeyed the commandment of God by marrying women of foreign nations whom God had forbidden his people to marry, women who eventually caused him to backslide. There is a great possibility that he died in disobedience to God.

Additionally, a person in leadership position must be an example of faithfulness and holy living. Paul commanded, *"A bishop then must be blameless,* **the husband of one wife***, vigilant, sober, of good* *behavior, given to hospitality, apt to teach; Not given to wine, no striker, not greedy of filthy lucre; but patient, not a brawler, not covetous."* 1 (Timothy 2:2-3) Living a virtuous life is a must for those in leadership, for when they fall, they usually carry a whole lot of people with them. **We must remember that no one, no matter how anointed or spiritually gifted is above God's word.**

God has raised the spiritual bar of purity higher as we passed into the new millennium. In order to hurdle this bar, Saints will have to let go and let God. **They will have to humble themselves to the ground.** It will be the only way. So Beloved, I entreat with you, let go of the presuppositions and opinions that conflict with God's word. Let go of the fears that challenge your faith in God. Marriage has always been close to God's heart because it demonstrates his closeness and unfailing love for his people. He will not allow marriage to be degraded to just an emotional or sexual experience. This is what the world wants marriage to be. *"If I'm not happy, I'm out. If the sex isn't good, I'm out!"* I assure you that God will punish all covenant breakers.

Remember Jesus' Sermon on the Mount, *"Not everyone that saith unto me, Lord, Lord, shall enter into the kingdom of heaven; but he that doeth the will of my Father which is in heaven. Many will say to me in that day, Lord, Lord, have we not prophesied in thy name? And in thy name have cast out devils? And in thy name done many wonderful words? And then will I profess unto them I never knew you depart from me, ye that work iniquity."* (Matthew 7:21-23) Forgiveness and humility are signs that the kingdom of God has come to a person's heart. A heart that is saturated with God's love will always forgive and seek reconciliation. This is the way of the Lord.

"Therefore if thou bring thy gift to the altar, and there rememberest that thy brother hath aught against thee; Leave there thy gift before the altar, and go thy way; first be reconciled to thy brother, and then come and offer thy gift." - Matthew 5:23-24

About The Authors

Lambert and Kim Sands are ministers of hope and encouragement to marriages and relationships through a ministry called Marriage Mechanics. They have been married for more than twenty-seven years, and have been in ministry for almost thirty-five years. The have three children. The couple, originally from the Bahamas, presently lives in Deltona, Florida. Lambert and Kim reach out to the hearts of others with a word that is open, honest and Biblical. They are gifted speakers, and the authors of numerous books. They are also the hosts of Marriage Mechanics TV program. Their ministry reaches out to build the family, community, church, and ultimately the nations.

For more information email us at:
marriagemechanics@hotmail.com

Telephone:
407 385 8201

Or visit us on the worldwide web:
www.marriagemechanics.org

Other Books Available:

'Latest publication: The Power of Submission'

Walking in Male Authority

Her Feminine Side

Living Single

The Price of Dominion

I'm in Charge…Right?

Understanding Why We Fuss & Fight

Victory in the Bedroom

Fight for Your Marriage

Why Cancer Doesn't Scare Me Anymore!

The Treasure Box (Devotional)

The Noah Chronicles

Overcoming Jezebel, Delilah & Anger

www.ingramcontent.com/pod-product-compliance
Lightning Source LLC
Chambersburg PA
CBHW031429290426
44110CB00011B/582